MURDER BY NATURAL CAUSES

A Full-Length Play
By
TIM KELLY

Adapted from the
murder mystery by
RICHARD LEVINSON
& WILLIAM LINK.

THE DRAMATIC PUBLISHING COMPANY

*** NOTICE ***

The amateur and stock acting rights to this work are controlled exclusively by THE DRAMATIC PUBLISHING COMPANY without whose permission in writing no performance of it may be given. Royalty fees are given in our current catalogue and are subject to change without notice. Royalty must be paid every time a play is performed whether or not it is presented for profit and whether or not admission is charged. A play is performed any time it is acted before an audience. All inquiries concerning amateur and stock rights should be addressed to:

DRAMATIC PUBLISHING
P. O. Box 129, Woodstock, Illinois 60098.

COPYRIGHT LAW GIVES THE AUTHOR OR THE AUTHOR'S AGENT THE EXCLUSIVE RIGHT TO MAKE COPIES. This law provides authors with a fair return for their creative efforts. Authors earn their living from the royalties they receive from book sales and from the performance of their work. Conscientious observance of copyright law is not only ethical, it encourages authors to continue their creative work. This work is fully protected by copyright. No alterations, deletions or substitutions may be made in the work without the prior written consent of the publisher. No part of this work may be reproduced or transmitted in any form or by any means, electronic or mechanical, including photocopy, recording, videotape, film, or any information storage and retrieval system, without permission in writing from the publisher. It may not be performed either by professionals or amateurs without payment of royalty. All rights, including but not limited to the professional, motion picture, radio, television, videotape, foreign language, tabloid, recitation, lecturing, publication, and reading are reserved. *On all programs this notice should appear:*

"Produced by special arrangement with
THE DRAMATIC PUBLISHING COMPANY of Woodstock, Illinois"

©MCMLXXXV by
TIM KELLY, LTD.

Based upon the teleplay,
NATURAL CAUSES

Printed in the United States of America
All Rights Reserved
(MURDER BY NATURAL CAUSES)

ISBN 0-87129-850-3

MURDER BY NATURAL CAUSES

A Play In Two Acts
For Four Women and Four Men

CHARACTERS

GIL WESTON .... young actor
ALLISON SINCLAIR .... Arthur's wife
ARTHUR SINCLAIR .... mentalist
GEORGE BRUBAKER .... Arthur's attorney
JESSICA PRESCOTT .... book editor
MARTA .... the Sinclairs' maid
EDDIE OAKMAN .... private investigator
MRS. CARRINGTON .... concert promoter

TIME: The present

PLACE: The study of Arthur Sinclair's home in Beverly Hills, California

ACT ONE

SCENE: *A warm, comfy, masculine study, very expensively furnished with framed posters of famous illusionists (e.g. Houdini) decorating the walls. The room is equipped with a bar and a fancy console with tape recording equipment. DR there is a doorway leading to an "inner-den." An entrance to the rest of the house is UR and French doors are L, leading to the garden.*

AT RISE OF CURTAIN: *The room is in darkness. The drapes are drawn across the French doors. We hear the taped voice of ARTHUR SINCLAIR.*

ARTHUR'S VOICE. A good many years ago, Houdini, the world's greatest escape artist and debunker of fake spiritualists, and Dunninger, the world's greatest mentalist, had dinner together in a restaurant. When they finished, they went back to Dunninger's car. But unfortunately the doors were locked. Do you know what happened? Houdini couldn't pick the lock and Dunninger couldn't remember where he put the keys. That story comes to mind whenever I begin to think I'm infallible...

(ALLISON enters UR.)

ALLISON. So this is where you're hiding. In the dark.
GIL. Uh-huh. *(ALLISON flicks a switch and immediately some lights snap on. GIL WESTON is stretched out on the sofa. He wears a stylish robe.)*
ARTHUR'S VOICE *(continuing from the console)*... still, we must continue to seek out answers.
ALLISON. Turn that cassette off.
GIL. I like listening to him.
ALLISON. I don't.

GIL. It's fascinating.
ALLISON. Not to me. (*She moves to the console.*)
ARTHUR'S VOICE. We must ask ourselves, "Is mind-reading possible"? Is there such a thing as a *sixth sense*? Does man survive death? Can we truly look into the future? (*ALLISON snaps off machine. ARTHUR's voice is silenced.*)
GIL (*lightly*). Why did you do that? I like to hear your husband ramble on.
ALLISON. I thought you were in the kitchen for a sandwich.
GIL (*standing*). I decided to come in here instead.
ALLISON (*checking her wristwatch*). I can catch him before he goes on. He'd like that. (*She moves to telephone, dials. GIL moves to bar, gets bottle of beer from refrigerator, opens it, sips, watches ALLISON in action as she speaks into phone.*) Hello. This is Mrs. Arthur Sinclair. Who am I speaking to please? (*Listens, puts her hand over mouthpiece, speaks to GIL.*) It's one of the production assistants. (*Into receiver.*) Would you get my husband. He's probably in the "Green Room." Oh, he is? Fine. (*Hands over mouthpiece, to GIL.*) He's about to go on. (*Pause. She waits for her husband's voice on the other end of the line.*) Arthur? It's me. Allison. I know you haven't much time. Just wanted to say I miss you. How do you feel? It's ticking nicely? Good. Keep it that way. I'll pick you up tomorrow at the airport. Love you. Good luck on the show. (*She hangs up, smiles at GIL across the room.*) How was I?
GIL. Not bad.
ALLISON. You approve?
GIL (*moving in front of bar*). Very convincing.
ALLISON. I'm always convincing.
GIL. Makes me wonder about the times *we* talk on the phone.
ALLISON (*amused*). Why darling, you almost sound insecure.
GIL (*putting his beer on the bar and moving to console*). Might as well turn on the TV.

Act I MURDER BY NATURAL CAUSES Page 7

ALLISON. What on earth for?

GIL (*surprised*). You're not going to watch your husband on the "Marty Chambers Show"? Watch him guess what's on people's minds? Tell them what they're thinking?

ALLISON. Marty Chambers is an egomaniac. That's why he makes such a good TV host. Why would I want to watch him? And never mind about Arthur. (*She moves toward sofa.*) He may be a world-famous mentalist, but the important thing is, right now he's five hundred miles away.

GIL (*reaching into pocket of robe, taking out and checking an empty cigarette pack*). You got any cigarettes? I'm all out.

ALLISON. You smoke too much.

GIL. I'm not the one with the bad heart.

ALLISON (*motioning GIL to her, invitingly*). Over here. I'm getting lonesome. (*GIL walks to her. They embrace, kiss.*) I like you in his bathrobe. (*Another kiss.*) Are you staying tonight?

GIL. Can't. All-day rehearsal tomorrow. I need sleep. (*Looks back toward console.*) He must be on by now. Suppose he asks you about the show.

ALLISON. I'll see it later.

GIL. You're recording it?

ALLISON (*pointing to DR door*). In there. House rule. Whenever he's on television, I have to videotape it. For posterity. Posterity is very important to Arthur. I suspect he thinks future archaeologists will one day dig up those videotapes and be impressed.

GIL. Doesn't his *gift* get under your skin?

ALLISON. I know all about his *gift*. (*Pause.*) At least I *think* I do. A few times he has startled me, but nothing I can't handle.

GIL (*nervously digging again at the cigarette pack*). I do need a cigarette. I'll quit next week.

ALLISON. You're supposed to be in training.

GIL. For what?

ALLISON (*forcefully*). For what? For next Friday night.

Don't tell me you've forgotten? (*GIL doesn't care for the trend in conversation, turns away, glumly.*)
GIL. I didn't make any promises.
ALLISON. But you're thinking about it?
GIL (*hesitating*). Yes.
ALLISON. That's good enough for now. Why don't you get me a drink.
GIL. White wine?
ALLISON. Naturally.
GIL (*crossing behind bar, talking as he goes*). I hate to say it, but your husband's good. I must have seen him half a dozen times. I can't figure out how he does it. (*He gets a small goblet and then a wine bottle, pours.*) Funny thing is, he's as much an actor as I am.
ALLISON. I've never thought of Arthur as an actor. (*She moves to antique table, opens drawer, takes out small handgun.*)
GIL. I don't understand how he can read someone's mind without working with a partner.
ALLISON. Why worry about it?
GIL. I'm not worried. I'm fascinated. (*ALLISON moves downstage, hand holding gun by her side. Gun seen by audience, but not by GIL.*) I mean... those old con games you hear about in carnivals and night clubs always had two people working together. They knew a code. (*Almost to himself.*) It has to be a code.
ALLISON. Never mind about the drink.
GIL. Huh?
ALLISON. Come here, Gil.
GIL. Another kiss?
ALLISON. You object?
GIL. I aim to please.
ALLISON (*holding gun tightly*). So do I. (*GIL swiftly steps from behind bar and crosses toward ALLISON. When GIL reaches the sofa, ALLISON raises the gun and aims point-blank at him.*)
GIL (*shocked and unbelieving*). Allison! (*ALLISON fires. GIL flings up hands, reels away, horrified, gradually realizing he hasn't been hurt.*)
ALLISON (*smiling at his reaction*). One more for good

Act I MURDER BY NATURAL CAUSES Page 9

measure. (*She points the gun toward the ceiling and fires again.*)
GIL (*angrily now*). What are you doing! Have you gone crazy? (*He steps to her, snatches the gun.*)
ALLISON (*matter-of-factly*). I hope you didn't put any ice in my drink. (*She crosses to the bar, takes the goblet, sips. GIL glares at her, still shaken. He examines the gun.*) It's empty. I only loaded two blanks.
GIL (*coldly*). What are you trying to prove?
ALLISON. Think, Gil. Two shots. Do you hear the phone ringing?
GIL. No.
ALLISON. Is anyone pounding on the front door or pushing the bell?
GIL. No.
ALLISON. Then I've made my point.
GIL (*smoldering*). I'm still not following.
ALLISON. Don't be dense. The sound doesn't carry beyond this house.
GIL. How do you know your neighbors aren't calling the police?
ALLISON. Because I've tried it before. (*Takes another sip.*) How's your heart?
GIL. Pounding.
ALLISON. Exactly.
GIL (*turning suddenly, steps to desk, slams down gun*). There has to be some other way.
ALLISON. There isn't. (*She moves to the sofa with the goblet, sits.*) It's a perfect plan. I've worked out every detail. No margin for error. I took the gun from my bedside table and moved it down here. (*Indicates antique table.*) That's where you find it when it's *time*.
GIL. You can divorce him.
ALLISON. We've already been over that. Arthur's gotten *extremely* rich in the past few years. Mumbo jumbo pays big bucks. Do you have any idea what his videotapes are worth? Not just in television syndication but in stores? People buy them like records. A gold

mine. Each and every one. Even his lectures. He's *preserved* for future generations. Future royalties.

GIL. He's a good businessman.

ALLISON. Arthur has a good attorney. The best. *He's* the businessman. I'm the vice-president in Arthur's corporation... "Sinclair, Inc." Did you know that?

GIL. You've mentioned it.

ALLISON. I'm a greedy little girl.

GIL (*turning*). Okay, fine. Be greedy. I'm all for greed. Take half the community property.

ALLISON (*putting goblet on table*). I don't want *half*. I want it all. Plus the insurance money.

GIL (*mumbling*). It won't work.

ALLISON. It *will* work. (*Sullenly, GIL drops into the chair in front of the desk.*) Gil, look at me. (*He doesn't.*) I said... look at me. (*GIL turns. She stands and moves slowly toward him.*) I've never pretended with you. I'm not sweet and I'm not innocent. I like to live well. If you wanted someone to bring home to mother, you should have found somebody else.

GIL. You're a cold-blooded lady.

ALLISON (*teasingly*). Am I? Sooner or later you'll have to decide. Darling, we can have it all. It's so easy.

GIL. Piece of cake, right? Falling off a log.

ALLISON. It can be. Gil...do you want me?

GIL. You know I do.

ALLISON. Then help me. Please. Think of yourself. You like wearing his robe; being in his house. (*Gestures to the room.*) Pretending all this is yours. Ours. (*She steps behind him, fools with his hair.*)

GIL. Look. This play I'm rehearsing at the Workshop Theatre. It's not much, but it's a showcase. If I'm lucky it can open things up. Not just commercials, but guest shots and maybe a TV series. I'm that good.

ALLISON. I believe you.

GIL. All that means *money*. Do you know what I'm saying?

ALLISON (*ahead of him*). I think so. (*GIL pulls away, stands.*)

GIL. But you're not buying.

Act I   MURDER BY NATURAL CAUSES   Page 11

ALLISON. Gil, you're a creative man.

GIL. Better believe it.

ALLISON (*moving back for her wine goblet, picks it up*). But to get up in the morning, you have to convince yourself that the next job, the next phone call, or the next showcase is going to change your life.

GIL. What's wrong with that?

ALLISON. It may be necessary to keep a struggling young actor going, but it hints of delusion.

GIL (*offended*). Delusion! (*Angrily.*) I like the way you give me a vote of confidence.

ALLISON. Darling, I want you to be successful. You will be. Maybe you're right. Maybe this play will do it for you.

GIL. I'm going to be great in it. You'll see.

ALLISON. I don't doubt it for a minute. But what if it fails? What if it doesn't turn out the way you expect? How long am I supposed to wait?

GIL (*moving toward her*). Allison, I can do a lot of things. I've *done* a lot of things.

ALLISON. Then what's worrying you?

GIL. I'm not sure I can kill someone. I'm not sure I can *murder* your husband.

ALLISON. But you have killed someone.

GIL (*amazed*). What are you talking about?

ALLISON (*putting down the goblet, stepping right*). The play. (*Folding her arms, she speaks as if instructing a backward pupil.*) You told me your character murders his wife.

GIL. That's right. With a syringe. That's a performance.

ALLISON (*intensely*). That's all I'm asking for. A *performance*. The only difference is that you'll have an audience of one. Think, Gil; everything you've ever wanted. No more stuggling; no more put downs from casting directors and studio secretaries. No more one-room apartments. No more driving around in a beat up Volks. You can have it all. Including me. (*Emphasizing each word.*) You... can... have... it... all. (*As she speaks, she moves back to him.*) All you have to do is reach out and take. All you have to do is give the performance of your life. (*She starts to kiss him, but he holds her off. She's surprised.*) Are you saying no?

GIL. I think we should wait a while.

ALLISON (*critically*). You do.

GIL. Why rush it?

ALLISON. I thought you were strong enough to play for high stakes. Obviously I was mistaken. You'd better leave, Gil.

GIL. Look, I'm sorry.

ALLISON. So am I.

GIL. Listen to me--

ALLISON. Why should I?

GIL. Because I'm asking you to. This doesn't have to change things. I mean, with us. We can go on just like we've been doing.

ALLISON. I said you'd better leave.

GIL (*almost a plea*). Allison.

ALLISON. Now.

GIL (*giving her a long stare, wanting to say more, deciding against it*). Have it your way. (*He strides UR.*)

ALLISON. Haven't you forgotten something?

GIL (*stopping, turning back*). What?

ALLISON. That robe. It doesn't belong to you. You couldn't *afford* it. (*GIL quickly removes the robe, puts it down somewhere appropriate and exits. ALLISON watches him depart as the curtain falls.*)

SCENE TWO

AT RISE OF CURTAIN: *It is a few days later. The French doors stand open and sunlight floods into the room. A large floral arrangement has been placed on the table behind the sofa. Now and again, from the grounds, we can hear the voices of guests. A garden party is in progress. DR door also stands open. ARTHUR SINCLAIR sits behind the desk. His attorney, GEORGE BRUBAKER, sits in front of the desk. He bites*

Act I MURDER BY NATURAL CAUSES Page 13

on a pipe. ARTHUR is checking over a legal document, quickly flipping the pages. Upstage, glancing at the books and the posters, is JESSICA PRESCOTT, dressed in chic businesswoman fashion.

ARTHUR. You've done it again, George. These contracts are totally incomprehensible.
GEORGE. Contracts are supposed to be incomprehensible. If you could understand them you wouldn't need an attorney.
ARTHUR. What do I do?
JESSICA. You sign them. (*She moves right of sofa.*)
GEORGE. Listen to Ms. Prescott, Arthur.
ARTHUR. Ms. Prescott is a book editor. When it comes to legal advice, I look to you.
GEORGE. In that case...sign.
ARTHUR. Committing myself to...
JESSICA. Three books over the next thirty-six months.
ARTHUR. One a year.
JESSICA. Roughly... although we want to rush the first one into print as soon as possible. There's a bookseller's convention in a few months. We want to push as many celebrity authors as we can.
ARTHUR. Books on mentalism aren't romance novels. I can't spit them out.
GEORGE. Ignore him, Ms. Prescott. Arthur likes to play his games. We're at his mercy. (*To ARTHUR.*) Sign.
ARTHUR. When's the deadline?
JESSICA. Yesterday.
ARTHUR. I don't write fast and I don't want to put anything out that's less than perfect.
GEORGE. No one's suggesting that you be another Tolstoy.
JESSICA. You've got the drafts of the first two books completed. All the lead-off book needs is some polishing and *punching up*. Leave that to me.
ARTHUR (*lightly*). Punching up? That sounds dangerous, Jessica.

Page 14 MURDER BY NATURAL CAUSES Act I

GEORGE. Think about the advance. If you have any doubts, that ought to erase them.
ARTHUR. How much?
JESSICA. Your attorney strikes a hard bargain.
ARTHUR (to GEORGE). What did you get me?
GEORGE. How does this sound - an advance of five hundred thousand dollars. (*Greatly pleased, ARTHUR gives a long, low whistle.*) I thought you'd like that.
JESSICA. The largest advance we've made this season.
ARTHUR. Five hundred thousand dollars. Hmmmmm. Nice.
GEORGE. You know you're going to commit yourself to the books. Wild dinosaurs couldn't stop you from signing that contract.
ARTHUR. You know me so well, George.
GEORGE. After all these years, is that so surprising?
ARTHUR. Comforting. (*He picks up a pen, toys with it. GEORGE and JESSICA are motionless, fearing he might "play" some more. ARTHUR thinks, smiles, then signs last page of contract.*) Signed, sealed and delivered. (*He holds out the contract. GEORGE and JESSICA exchange smiles. GEORGE stands, takes the contract, folds it, slips it inside his jacket. ARTHUR stands.*) Let's have a drink on it. (*He moves behind the bar.*) What'll it be?
GEORGE. Why don't you read my mind?
ARTHUR (to GEORGE). You, too? It's a conspiracy.
JESSICA. Y'know, I've never seen you in action. *In person*. It's always been on television.
GEORGE. Go on. Show her what you can do.
JESSICA. I've got a front row seat. (*ARTHUR throws up his hands in a gesture of resignation. JESSICA quickly sits in the chair DR as if she were a theatre patron. She studies ARTHUR from on the edge of the chair. ARTHUR steps in front of the bar, rubbing his chin.*)
ARTHUR. Let me concentrate. Hmmm. Yes. You usually drink brandy, but I get the impression of - scotch on the rocks.
GEORGE. That's correct.
JESSICA. Marvelous.

Act I   MURDER BY NATURAL CAUSES   Page 15

ARTHUR. Thank you, Jessica. Are you impressed, George?
GEORGE. Not really. Considering we had dinner last week and I told you I was switching to scotch.
ARTHUR. I'm hurt. Are you saying you doubt my powers?
JESSICA. He certainly can't doubt your earning powers.
ARTHUR. True. I've suddenly become *marketable*. No question about that. It's the age we live in. People still want miracles.
JESSICA. Is that what you're in - the miracle business?
ARTHUR. Oh, I dress it up with words like telepathy, precognition and E.S.P. Everyone suspects I'm a fraud of course, but they're not quite sure. That's what fascinates them - the fact that I might be legitimate.
GEORGE. Puts you under a lot of pressure, doesn't it?
ARTHUR. You know me. It's nothing I can't handle.
GEORGE. How are you feeling?
ARTHUR *(to JESSICA)*. He's getting as bad as Allison. *(To GEORGE.)* My coronary was two years ago. Ancient history. *(Taps his chest.)* I've got an expensive little box in my chest that doesn't miss a beat. And I can still swamp you at tennis. Okay?
GEORGE *(laughing)*. Okay.
JESSICA. I must say I'm disappointed in my *in person* demonstration.
ARTHUR *(to GEORGE)*. They always want more.

(MARTA, the Sinclair's maid, in uniform, enters L through the French doors. She carries an empty hors d'oeuvres tray.)

MARTA. Your wife wants to know how much longer you're going to be, Mr. Sinclair. The guests are asking for you.
ARTHUR. Anticipation is ninety percent of pleasure. *(To JESSICA.)* Watch. (He crosses and takes the tray from MARTA, hands it to GEORGE, who places it on the desk. ARTHUR pulls MARTA in front of the sofa.)

MARTA. Oh, Mr. Sinclair, you're not going to read my mind again?

ARTHUR. It'll be painless.

MARTA. It's embarrassing when you read my mind. I'm never thinking of anything.

ARTHUR. Sssssssh.

MARTA. Can't you do something, Mr. Brubaker?

GEORGE. I wouldn't dare interfere. He might put a hex on me.

ARTHUR (*looking to JESSICA, then to MARTA*). I want you each to think of your first name.

MARTA. First name?

ARTHUR. That's right.

MARTA. I'm thinking.

ARTHUR. Are you thinking, Ms. Prescott?

JESSICA. I am.

ARTHUR. Good. Now count the number of letters in your first name.

JESSICA. Done.

ARTHUR. You do the same, Marta. (*To JESSICA.*) Your first name is Jessica.

GEORGE. You didn't have to read her mind for that.

ARTHUR. Jessica has eight letters and Marta has five. Ready?

JESSICA. Ready.

MARTA (*uncomfortably*). Ready.

ARTHUR (*slowly, professionally*). Now add the number ten - that's ten plus the number of letters in your first name.

JESSICA. Done.

ARTHUR. Next, subtract two. Next, add three. Finally, subtract your original number. Got it? (*Both women nod. ARTHUR puts his fingertips to his temples.*) The number you are thinking of, Jessica, and the number you are thinking of, Marta... hmmmmm...

GEORGE. Having trouble?

ARTHUR. It isn't that. It's an extraordinary coincidence because they've both come up with the same two-digit number. And that number is... eleven.

JESSICA (*amazed*). That's extraordinary. Yes. Eleven.

Act I MURDER BY NATURAL CAUSES Page 17

ARTHUR. Was I on target, Marta?

MARTA. How should I know? I'm no good at arithmetic. (*She moves toward exit UR.*)

ARTHUR. That's a wonderful idea, Marta. Nice of you to think of it.

MARTA (*stopping*). Think of what, Mr. Sinclair?

ARTHUR. You were going to ask me if I wouldn't like some of your delicious hors d'oeuvres. Freshly made.

MARTA. I was?

ARTHUR. You were.

MARTA. Would you like some of my delicious hors d'oeuvres? Freshly made.

ARTHUR (*slapping his hands in glee*). There! What did I tell you.

MARTA (*a funny look on her face*). I wish you'd stay out of my head, Mr. Sinclair. (*She suspects she's been fooled, but doesn't know how.*) There's barely room enough for me up there. (*She exits UR.*)

JESSICA (laughing). Poor Marta. She's no match for you.

GEORGE. You shouldn't tease her, Arthur. Good servants aren't easy to find.

JESSICA. That business with the number, eleven. How did you do it?

ARTHUR. Professional secret.

GEORGE. What happened to my scotch on the rocks.

ARTHUR. Coming up. For you, Jessica?

JESSICA. Later.

(*ARTHUR moves behind the bar as ALLISON enters L through French doors. She "sweeps in" looking smashing in a hostess frock.*)

ALLISON (*to ARTHUR*). Arthur. What's keeping you? (*To GEORGE.*) George, you may be a good lawyer, but you're a bad influence on my husband. (*To ARTHUR.*) You're supposed to be circulating.

ARTHUR. Put on a videotape. They won't even know I'm missing.

JESSICA. I'm to blame for this conference, Mrs.

Sinclair. The publisher insisted. But I think you'll be pleased to know it's turned out splendidly.
ALLISON. Oh?
GEORGE. How does this sound, Allison? An advance of half-a-million dollars.
ALLISON (*impressed*). Half-a-million dollars? (*Steps C.*) That does sound *splendid*. (*To ARTHUR.*) Mrs. Carrington is waiting for you. She's getting restless.
ARTHUR (*playfully*). Mrs. Carrington? Mrs. Carrington? Ah, yes, the woman who books the charity and concert affairs.
ALLISON. And always with heavy publicity.
GEORGE. I'm told she can be difficult.
ALLISON. Only because she won't buy unless she's completely satisfied she has something special to offer the public.
GEORGE. Convince Mrs. Carrington, Arthur.
ALLISON. She's half-convinced already, but she's impatient. (*To ARTHUR.*) You don't want to let her off the hook.
GEORGE. Allison here would make a first-rate agent.
ALLISON. Perish the thought.
JESSICA. A one-man tour would make a great tie-up for the new books.
ALLISON. There you have it, Arthur. Mrs. Carrington is money in the vault.
ARTHUR. I don't know if I want to do a tour.
GEORGE. Come along, Ms. Prescott. We'll leave these two to squabble it out. I'll introduce you to some people who'll be interested in buying Arthur's new book.
JESSICA. By all means.
ALLISON (*to GEORGE*). Arthur has every intention of doing a tour.
ARTHUR. What about your drink?
GEORGE. It'll keep. (*GEORGE and JESSICA exit L through French doors. GEORGE allows JESSICA to exit first, then follows.*)
ALLISON (*stepping to floral arrangement, fusses with blooms*). I hope you don't mind this garden party.

Act I MURDER BY NATURAL CAUSES Page 19

Mrs. Carrington is only in town for a few days. (*ALLISON turns. ARTHUR doesn't answer. He takes a crumpled cigarette pack from his pocket. It's the one from Scene One.*)
ARTHUR. What have you been up to?
ALLISON (*suddenly worried, recognizing the pack*). What do you mean?
ARTHUR. Where did this come from?
ALLISON. How should I know?
ARTHUR (*stepping toward her*). I found it in the pocket of my robe. (*Pause.*)
ALLISON (*smiling*). You caught me.
ARTHUR. Smoking again. Turning your palate to ash.
ALLISON. No will power. I've been sneaking them behind your back.
ARTHUR (*with a disappointed sigh*). Oh, Allison.
ALLISON. I promise I'll never have another cigarette.
ARTHUR. Scout's honor?
ALLISON (*crossing her heart, holding up a hand for a pledge*). Scout's honor.
ARTHUR (*something occurring to him*). Wait a minute.
ALLISON. Now what?
ARTHUR. Why were your cigarettes in the pocket of my robe? (*Pause as ALLISON realizes the danger she's in. She quickly recovers, moves in close.*)
ALLISON. Darling, promise you won't think I'm silly. (*Kisses him.*) You won't laugh.
ARTHUR. Depends.
ALLISON. You weren't here the other night, so I wore your robe to bed. I guess I wanted something of you - close to me.
ARTHUR. No wonder I love you so much. (*They embrace. Audience can see ALLISON'S face over his shoulder. She gives a soundless sigh of great relief.*)

(*MARTA enters UR.*)

MARTA. Oh, excuse me.
ALLISON (*pulling away from ARTHUR*). What is it, Marta?

MARTA. It's Mr. Oakman. (*To ARTHUR.*) Says he has to talk with you.
ARTHUR. About time. Tell him to come in.
MARTA. Yes, sir. (*She exits.*)
ARTHUR (*pushing ALLISON toward the grounds.*) You hold off Mrs. Carrington.
ALLISON. That won't be easy.
ARTHUR. You can do it.
ALLISON. I'll give it my best shot. Remember, Arthur, she's terribly important.
ARTHUR. Ah, money, money, money.
ALLISON. Duty calls. (*ALLISON exits L through French doors*).

(*From offstage, we hear some laughter or muted conversation from the unseen guests. ARTHUR steps to the French doors and pulls them shut, locking them. EDDIE OAKMAN enters UR.*)

EDDIE. Sorry I'm late.
ARTHUR. I expected you two hours ago.
EDDIE. My car broke down on the Pasadena Freeway. Have you ever broken down on the Pasadena Freeway?
ARTHUR. No, and I don't intend to. Why didn't you call in?
EDDIE. You know why. You got too many phone extensions in this house. Garden party going on. Someone could listen in.
ARTHUR. I hadn't thought of that.
EDDIE. I know my business, Mr. Sinclair.
ARTHUR. I won't give you an argument on that score. (*Looking off.*) I can see her out there. I can't stall her much longer.
EDDIE. If I didn't show up you could cover with some of your old stuff, couldn't you?
ARTHUR. No, I couldn't, Eddie. I'm on top because I keep everything moving. We're wasting time. What have you got? Give.
EDDIE. Okay if I sit?
ARTHUR. Sit, stand, only hurry up. And don't ask for

Act I   MURDER BY NATURAL CAUSES   Page 21

a drink. You're not staying. (*EDDIE sits on sofa, takes out a note pad, flips the cover to read.*)
EDDIE. I had to call Chicago. Got me a big phone bill on this one.
ARTHUR. Why do you care? I'll be paying for it.
EDDIE (*looking down at the note pad*). Here goes. This here Mrs. Carrington is having a gazebo built in back of her house. Contractor's name is Scofield.
ARTHUR. Got it. Keep going. (*As EDDIE continues, ARTHUR keeps one eye on the grounds, making sure they won't be interrupted.*)
EDDIE. This is a goodie. Mrs. Carrington's got this mutt. Whadda-ya-call 'em? Lhasa Assa? Lhasa Alpo? Something like that.
ARTHUR. Close. Lhasa Apso.
EDDIE. Anyway, his name is Toby and she took him to the vet last week. He's an old dog. Arthritis.
ARTHUR. Is there a Mr. Carrington?
EDDIE. Nope. Widow. Husband was a surgeon.
ARTHUR. What else?
EDDIE. She's always going on a diet and worries about her cholesterol count.
ARTHUR. More.
EDDIE. She's got a niece who ran away and joined a cult.
ARTHUR. What kind of cult?
EDDIE (*checking name*). Something called *Children of the Flowers*.
ARTHUR. That cult was dying the day it started. I give it another few months. I'm still listening.
EDDIE. She loves TV soap opera.
ARTHUR. Pass.
EDDIE. Her favorite food is baked potato with plenty of sour cream.
ARTHUR. Kid stuff.
EDDIE. She made some big real estate investments a few months back and she worries about them.
ARTHUR. Where?
EDDIE. Border country. Arizona.

ARTHUR. She can't miss. Real estate value there has shot up handsomely in the last few weeks.

(*MARTA enters UR.*)

MARTA. I hope I'm not disturbing you, Mr. Sinclair, but I think I left my tray in here.
ARTHUR. Tray? (*Remembering, looks to desk.*) Oh, yes. Here it is. (*He picks up tray, moves halfway upstage to meet MARTA, crossing down to meet him. EDDIE continues to study his notes.*)
MARTA (*concerned*). I know this isn't the time, Mr. Sinclair, but do you think your wife would mind if I took tomorrow evening off instead of Friday? It's my sister. She's giving a little party for my nephew. He's going into the Marines.
ARTHUR. I'm certain she won't mind. I know I don't.
MARTA (*turning to exit UR, stopping, looking back*). I don't know why I have to ask you anything. You always know what's on my mind before I do. (*She exits UR.*)
EDDIE. You got another fan there, Mr. Sinclair.
ARTHUR. I cherish each and every one. That wrap it up?
EDDIE. It's the best I could do on this one. If I had more time...
ARTHUR. I didn't know my wife was going to spring Mrs. Carrington on me.
EDDIE (*standing*). If you need me, you know how to reach me.
ARTHUR. Thanks again, Eddie. I owe you one.
EDDIE. You don't owe me anything, Mr. Sinclair. I owe you.
ARTHUR. Let's not hear that again.
EDDIE (*ignoring the request*). People won't hire an ex-drunk. A private investigator on the bottle is bad news. If you hadn't given me a chance I'd be down and out for the count.
ARTHUR. I employ you because you're the best at what you do. You are being discreet?

Act I MURDER BY NATURAL CAUSES Page 23

EDDIE. You know me, Mr. Sinclair. I'm the invisible man. Now you see him, now you don't. (*EDDIE exits UR. ARTHUR unlocks the French doors and opens them wide. He looks for ALLISON, catches her eye in the near-distance, waves. He nods and motions as if to say it's all right to come in. Briskly, he then moves across the room and exits DR into the inner den, closing the door after him.*)

MRS. CARRINGTON'S VOICE (*from grounds*). I can't wait to meet your husband. Quite exciting.

ALLISON'S VOICE (*from grounds*). He's anxious to meet you, Mrs. Carrington.

MRS. CARRINGTON'S VOICE. How nice.

(*MRS. CARRINGTON enters L through French doors. ALLISON follows her into the room.*)

MRS. CARRINGTON. Your husband does know that I book only the best concert attractions.

ALLISON. Naturally.

MRS. CARRINGTON. The best don't always turn out to be the most profitable, but I wouldn't think of booking anything shabby or second-rate.

ALLISON. Arthur is not shabby nor second-rate.

MRS. CARRINGTON. Oh, my dear, I didn't mean to imply...

ALLISON. I understand. (*Gestures to sofa.*) Won't you sit down?

MRS. CARRINGTON. Thank you. (*She sits.*)

(*The door to the inner-den opens and ARTHUR steps in. He strikes a pose. This is his "entrance." He puts his fingertips to his temples.*)

ARTHUR. The answer to your question, Mrs. Carrington, is *yes*.

MRS. CARRINGTON (*startled*). Who? What? (*Seeing him, she relaxes.*) Oh, it's you, Mr. Sinclair. (*ALLISON steps up right of desk.*) What question?

ARTHUR. The one you were just thinking.

Page 24   MURDER BY NATURAL CAUSES   Act I

MRS. CARRINGTON (*smiling*). That's clever of you. Especially, since I don't know what I was thinking. (*Both ALLISON and ARTHUR look disappointed. MRS. CARRINGTON is nobody's fool. ARTHUR moves to sofa.*)
MRS. CARRINGTON. It's all psychology, isn't it?
ARTHUR. Perhaps. And then again, perhaps not.
MRS. CARRINGTON. Psychology and manipulation. Something like reading Tarot cards. You meet the person, get a feeling for his personality and go from there.
ARTHUR. Mentalism has nothing in common with Tarot cards.
MRS. CARRINGTON (*testing him*). Can you really read my mind?
ARTHUR. Are you sure you want me to?
MRS. CARRINGTON. I have no dark secrets.
ARTHUR (*fingertips to temples*). As you wish. (*ALLISON sitting in front of desk, watches.*) Concentrate, please. (*MRS. CARRINGTON concentrates.*) You're a widow. Your husband was a doctor - a surgeon.
MRS. CARRINGTON. Hardly a revelation, Mr. Sinclair.
ARTHUR. Patience. (*Stepping closer.*) I'm afraid this is quite personal. There's a new man in your life.
MRS. CARRINGTON. Is that a fact?
ARTHUR. Perhaps I shouldn't continue.
MRS. CARRINGTON. I insist.
ARTHUR. No, wait. You have been spending a great deal of time with him, but I sense it's perfectly innocent. His name is - Scofield.
MRS. CARRINGTON. Scofield?!
ALLISON. Perhaps it's something *like* Scofield.
MRS. CARRINGTON. No, no, Scofield is right. He's my...
ARTHUR (*interrupting smoothly*). Your contractor.
MRS. CARRINGTON. How on earth...
ARTHUR. He's building something for your yard. A pool? No, some kind of wooden structure. Picture it in your mind, please. (*MRS. CARRINGTON closes her eyes, concentrates.*) Would it be - a gazebo?

Act I   MURDER BY NATURAL CAUSES   Page 25

MRS. CARRINGTON (*opening her eyes, amazed*). Yes, it would. (*To ALLISON.*) How could you possibly keep any secrets?
ALLISON. I never have secrets from my husband.
ARTHUR (*still "on"*). I see a wet nose. I get the name - Toby. (*MRS. CARRINGTON is mesmerized.*) Is it a child?
MRS. CARRINGTON. No.
ARTHUR. A dog. You're worried about your dog.
MRS. CARRINGTON. Yes. Yes, I am.
ARTHUR. Don't be. It's only a touch of arthritis. He'll survive quite nicely.
MRS. CARRINGTON. I'm not sure I want you to go on.
ARTHUR. Don't worry about your female relative. A niece, perhaps?
MRS. CARRINGTON (hesitatingly). Yes. My niece.
ARTHUR. Whatever *force* is holding her. It will soon be disbanded.
MRS. CARRINGTON. That's comforting.
ARTHUR. I also get the *impression* of the desert. Desert land. You're involved in some way. Financially. Don't worry. That desert sand will turn to gold.
MRS. CARRINGTON (*ecstatically*). Enough. (*Stands.*) I don't know how you do it, Mr. Sinclair. I don't want to know. You could be a warlock or a wizard. If we can work out the terms I think I can assure you of a most profitable tour. I thought the billing might read: "Arthur Sinclair, The Man From Whom You Cannot Keep A Secret." Do you like that?
ARTHUR. What do you think, Allison?
ALLISON. Wonderful.
MRS. CARRINGTON. I understand you videotape all your television appearances.
ARTHUR. Never miss.
MRS. CARRINGTON. I'd like to see some of them when it's convenient.
ARTHUR. What better time than now? (*Indicates inner-den.*) A giant screen and a comfortable seat. My private theatre. I'll start the machine for you.

MRS. CARRINGTON (*to ALLISON*). Your husband doesn't miss an opportunity, does he?

ALLISON. Seldom.

MRS. CARRINGTON. You're definitely a man of action. (*ARTHUR again gestures to the inner-den. MRS. CARRINGTON makes the cross.*)

MRS. CARRINGTON. "Arthur Sinclair, The Man From Whom You Cannot Keep A Secret." (*Envisioning success.*) "Sold out."

(*MRS. CARRINGTON exits DR to inner-den. ARTHUR turns to ALLISON, all smiles, clasps his hands together and holds them up like a winning prizefighter. He exits to inner-den. MARTA enters UR with hors d'oeuvres on a plate.*)

MARTA. These are just made, Mrs. Sinclair. Your husband wanted some.

ALLISON. Put them anywhere. (*MARTA puts tray on table behind sofa.*)

MARTA (*easing into it*). Mr. Sinclair said it would be all right if I took tomorrow evening off, instead of Friday.

ALLISON. Why?

MARTA. My nephew's going into the Marines. My sister's having a party for him. Quite a few relatives that I haven't seen for some time.

ALLISON. Take a couple of days, Marta.

MARTA (*overwhelmed*). You mean it?

ALLISON. You deserve a little holiday. It'll do you good.

MARTA. I appreciate it. (*She moves UR.*)

ALLISON. Marta?

MARTA (*turning*). Yes, Mrs. Sinclair?

ALLISON. The afternoon paper - is it here yet?

MARTA. Yes. It's in the hallway. Do you want it?

ALLISON. Please.

Act I   MURDER BY NATURAL CAUSES   Page 27

(MARTA exits UR. ARTHUR enters DR from the inner-den.)

ARTHUR *(calling over his shoulder)*. I'll see if I can locate Mr. Brubaker.
MRS. CARRINGTON'S VOICE *(from inner-den)*. Do that. I want to meet him. *(ARTHUR closes the door, crosses to ALLISON rubbing his hands in glee.)*
ARTHUR *(softly)*. She's not eating out of my hand, she's *lapping* it.
ALLISON. Get George and get something down on paper. You know my motto. "Strike while the iron's hot."
ARTHUR *(playfully)*. I didn't know that was your motto.
ALLISON. I hope you realize you're having a successful day.
ARTHUR. *We're* having a successful day.

(ALLISON smiles and ARTHUR exits L through French doors onto the grounds. MARTA enters UR with the newspaper.)

MARTA. Here's the paper.
ALLISON *(taking the paper)*. You might as well circulate with that tray before everything gets cold.
MARTA. Yes, Mrs. Sinclair. *(She gets the hors d'oeuvres tray from behind sofa and exits L through French doors. ALLISON walks to sofa, checking index on front of paper.)*
ALLISON *(reading aloud)*. "STAGE NEWS: NEW THRILLER OPENS LAST NIGHT. See entertainment section, page sixteen." *(She sits and hastily turns the pages.)* Sixteen... sixteen... sixteen. *(Finds it.)* Sixteen! *(Scanning the page she finds what she is looking for and reads aloud.)* "There may be such a thing as gifted amateurs, but they were not on display last night at the Workshop Theatre." *(She reads on silently, stops, lowers the newspaper. There's a thoughtful expression on her face. She looks toward the telephone, then toward the closed door of the inner-den.*

Page 28   MURDER BY NATURAL CAUSES   Act I

Newspaper in her grip, she stands, crosses to the inner-den door, opens it and pokes her head inside.) Do you need anything, Mrs. Carrington?
MRS. CARRINGTON'S VOICE *(from inside the room)*. I'm fine.
ALLISON. If you do need anything, just call.
MRS. CARRINGTON'S VOICE. I will. *(ALLISON closes the door and moves quickly to the French doors, looking out. She steps to the telephone. Putting down the newspaper, she dials, waits a moment for an answer.)*
ALLISON. Gil? It's Allison. I was afraid you wouldn't be answering your phone. Yes, I read the afternoon paper. That's why I'm calling. I know how depressed you get and I was worried. Listen, Gil, you're a talented young man. You've got a lot going for you. That critic doesn't know what she's talking about. Besides, it's only one critic's opinion. Gil? Are you listening to me? I'm planning on seeing the show tomorrow evening. Is that all right with you? It's already closed? One performance? Only one? I'm not rubbing it in. I'm crushed. I mean that. Have you been drinking or taken anything? You sound so strange. *(Coolly.)* I don't want to talk about that. I've changed my mind. You were quite right. There has to be another way. But that's my problem, not yours. I said I don't want to talk about it, no. *(Fast.)* Not over the phone, Gil. I won't listen. *(Looks toward door of inner-den, making sure MRS. CARRINGTON is not about to pop in.)* All right. I'll see you, if that's what *you* want. No, here. Tomorrow night. Arthur's going out of town. Don't come to the front door. *(She hangs up. Slowly a satisfied smile creeps across her lips. She looks like the cat that swallowed the canary. She picks up the theatre review with a great sense of satisfaction. Her smile widens.)* Strike while the iron is hot. *(She tosses the newspaper aside and exits L striding through the French doors to mingle with her guests. CURTAIN)*

Act I   MURDER BY NATURAL CAUSES   Page 29

SCENE THREE

AT RISE OF CURTAIN: *It is the following night. The lights glow softly, giving the room a comfy aura. The door to the inner-den stands open. Drapes at the closed French doors are pulled aside.*

ARTHUR'S VOICE (*offstage, UR*). Marta, if you want to ride with me you'd better hurry.
MARTA'S VOICE (*from inner-den*). Yes, yes, Mr. Sinclair. I'm coming.
ARTHUR'S VOICE (*offstage, UR*). Where are you?

(MARTA, wearing a thin topcoat and silly-looking hat enters DR from the inner-den, holding a photograph. ARTHUR enters UR, also wearing a topcoat.)

MARTA. I was getting one of your pictures, Mr. Sinclair. I promised my sister Alice I'd get you to autograph it for her.
ARTHUR. There are publicity pictures in the top drawer of the desk.
MARTA. But they're not glossies. My sister wants a glossy. (*Waves picture.*) It would cheer her up. She doesn't want my nephew to leave home.
ARTHUR. Okay, anything, so long as it gets you moving. I don't want to miss my flight. (*He takes the photograph from MARTA, moves quickly to desk. Picking up a pen he scrawls something across it.*)
ARTHUR (*tossing the pen aside, holding out the glossy.*) That ought to do it.
MARTA. My sister will be so pleased. (*She crosses to ARTHUR, takes the photograph, reading what he's written.*) "TO ALICE, AN OPEN MIND DOES NOT MEAN A HOLE IN THE HEAD. ARTHUR SINCLAIR." (*She smiles.*) She'll like that.
ARTHUR. Do you have a bag?
MARTA. My small one. It's in the hallway.

(ALLISON enters UR, looking at her wristwatch.)

ALLISON. Arthur, you'd better hurry.
MARTA. It's my fault, Mrs. Sinclair. I wanted a glossy.
(She exits hurriedly UR. ALLISON moves toward ARTHUR.)
ALLISON. I wish I felt up to driving you to the airport, but this terrible headache. I think it's the smog.
ARTHUR. No problem. I'll park the car in an overnight garage and it will be waiting for me in the morning. I've got to get busy on that first chapter. I promised Ms. Prescott. She wants it by the end of the week.
ALLISON. Sure you don't mind about driving out by yourself?
ARTHUR. Subject closed.
ALLISON *(smiling)*. Whatever you say.
ARTHUR. And you get over that headache.
ALLISON. I'll come to the door with you.

(They exit UR. A moment or two after they begin their upstage cross, we see GIL outside the French doors. He waits until they're gone, then steps inside the study. He doesn't look good. He's exhausted. His clothes are rumpled as if he's slept in them. Sitting in the desk chair, he searches his pocket for a cigarette, takes out a pack, shaking it. ALLISON enters UR.)

ALLISON *(stunned)*. Are you out of your mind?
GIL. I waited 'til he left.
ALLISON. What if he suddenly came back? What if he forgot something?
GIL. You'd think of something to say.
ALLISON *(pointing to inner-den)*. Get in there until I'm sure he's gone.
GIL *(irritated)*. Come on.
ALLISON. Do it.

(ALLISON exits UR. Annoyed, GIL crosses DR and exits into inner-den. The room remains empty. Another moment passes and ALLISON enters UR. She closes drapes then steps to door of inner-den.)

Act I   MURDER BY NATURAL CAUSES   Page 31

ALLISON (*calling*). You can come out. (*She steps to sofa, sits.*)

(*GIL enters DR from inner-den.*)

GIL (*with a touch of bitterness*). I can come out, huh? I've been a good boy. You make me feel like a well-trained Doberman.

ALLISON (*casually*). Why are you angry?

GIL. My reviews! (*He pulls some newspaper reviews, clipped together, from his pocket, shaking them at her.*)

ALLISON. I didn't write them.

GIL (*reading, almost snarling*). "There may be such a thing as gifted amateurs, but they were not on display last night at the Workshop Theatre."

ALLISON. I read that one.

GIL (*ignoring her, repeating*). "But they were *not* on display last night at the Workshop Theatre, nor was the audience. After the first intermission, they began to leave like rats deserting a sinking script." (*He takes a step toward ALLISON.*) Not ship. *Script.* Rats deserting a sinking script. Clever, huh?

ALLISON. No, it's not clever. It's cruel. Get rid of those things.

GIL (*flipping to another review.*) Wait, wait. They get better.

ALLISON. You're only tormenting yourself.

GIL (*angrily*). "Gil Weston, as the murderous doctor, is physically commanding..."

ALLISON. What's the matter with that?

GIL. "... but lacks the technique and suavity to carry an entire evening."

ALLISON. Oh.

GIL (*challenging*). Want to hear some more?

ALLISON. I don't think so. (*Shifting mood.*) Why don't I make some coffee?

GIL. I don't want any coffee.

ALLISON. Where did you park your car?

GIL. Don't worry. No one will see it.

ALLISON (*standing*). I'd like a cup.

GIL (*excitedly*). Forget about coffee. You were right. What you said the other night. About me and delusion.

ALLISON. I didn't mean it.

GIL. No? (*ALLISON walks to French doors, peering outside.*)

ALLISON. I've been thinking, maybe we should keep things the way they were.

GIL (*scoffing*). Back to square one?

ALLISON. That's what you said you wanted. It's nice. It's better than nice, it's safe.

GIL. Nice, and safe. If he doesn't get suspicious and you don't run out of excuses, we can sneak a few hours together from time to time. That's it, huh?

ALLISON (*turning*). I can live with that. Why can't you? (*ALLISON crosses to behind bar, gets two goblets, pouring some wine into each.*)

GIL. And every once in a while I can take you out to dinner. Someplace cheap, and nobody you know will see us together. That wouldn't do. Sorry. We've been there. (*He sits dejectedly on sofa.*)

ALLISON. I don't think I'm following you.

GIL. You're following me. Do you know why you let me come here tonight?

ALLISON. Because you sounded so desperate and lonely when I called.

GIL. No. You wanted to see if I've changed my mind about your husband.

ALLISON. That's not true.

GIL. Yes, it is. And it's okay. (*Pause.*) Because I have. (*ALLISON gives him a sharp look. Suddenly he jumps up, excited, his adrenalin speeding.*) I mean, why not? No more delusion. This time I don't get reviewed, I get rich. The performance of my life. Isn't that what you said? (*ALLISON crosses to him with the goblets, handing him one.*)

ALLISON (*calmly*). You're sure? You're absolutely sure? (*GIL moves to desk, eager to plot ARTHUR'S murder.*)

GIL. I get here at eight, right?

Act I MURDER BY NATURAL CAUSES Page 33

ALLISON. A few minutes before. I'll leave the door unlocked when I go out.

GIL. Be simpler if I ring the bell.

ALLISON. But not as effective. We want to keep him off-balance.

GIL. Friday?

ALLISON. No. I've given Marta two days off. The timing's too good to pass up. Arthur will be back on an early morning flight, so it's tomorrow night. Monday.

GIL. Remember that old nursery rhyme? (*As a child might recite.*) "Solomon Grundy died on Monday." Only it won't be Solomon Grundy, will it? It'll be Arthur Sinclair.

ALLISON. Don't be cute. It's not your style. (*GIL sits in desk chair. He goes "quiet."*)

GIL. One minor detail. (*He looks up at ALLISON.*) What do we do if it doesn't work?

ALLISON. We have the *contingency*.

GIL (*staring into his wine goblet*). Ah, yes. The *Resurrection*.

ALLISON. Second thoughts?

GIL. Wondering.

ALLISON. About what?

GIL (*looking at her*). A year from now. Rich, beautiful widow, beautiful estate. What stops you from cutting me loose?

ALLISON (*stepping to him*). Among other things, darling, you know too much. (*Lightly.*) I hate to give up that half-million dollar advance on those books. (*GIL looks startled.*) That's what he's getting from his publisher. (*Musing.*) Perhaps Ms. Prescott can salvage that for me. She's eager and bright. She might like to *ghost* the books.

GIL. Are you trying to be funny?

ALLISON. Not really. You are glum. This is a happy occasion, Gil. Everything you've ever wanted.

GIL. Except a decent review.

ALLISON. Will you forget about those? They're meaningless now.

GIL. All right. I'll think about something else. (*With a*

calculating tone.) I'll think about the fact I can't use what I have on you because I'd put myself in jail.

ALLISON (*brightly*). Then I suppose you'll just have to trust me, won't you?

GIL. I suppose.

ALLISON. I won't come into the house until I hear the shot. That will be eight-thirty, give or take a few minutes.

GIL. How are you loading the gun?

ALLISON. One blank and five live rounds. The blank in the chamber.

GIL. Unless you happen to forget.

ALLISON. Why would I forget?

GIL (*casually shrugging*). You might be tempted to kill two birds with one stone.

ALLISON (*growing angry*). Now look, if you don't trust me...

GIL. Sure I trust you. Like you said - I have to. Especially when that gun goes off.

ALLISON (*turning her back on him*). Maybe we should forget the whole thing.

GIL (*smiling*). Just testing. (*He stands.*) Let's toast the future.

ALLISON (*facing him, pleased*). The future.

GIL. So long as we both understand... it's *murder*.

ALLISON. Not murder, darling. Heart failure. Death by natural causes. (*She holds up goblet.*) Let's drink to the performance of your life. (*They clink glasses.*)

CURTAIN

ACT TWO

AT RISE OF CURTAIN: *It is Monday evening. The drapes are closed. MRS. CARRINGTON is seated in the DR chair. JESSICA is seated on the sofa, a large manila envelope by her side. GEORGE stands behind sofa. ARTHUR is seated behind desk.*

MRS. CARRINGTON. I know it's an imposition rushing things like this, but I've had a *big* name slip through my fingers more than once and I don't want to take any chances with you, Mr. Sinclair.

ARTHUR. You're for it, George. So is Allison. That makes it unanimous.

GEORGE. I've drawn up a temporary agreement. Mrs. Carrington has already signed. The details of your tour can be worked out at a later date. (*He opens his attache case which is on table behind sofa, taking out four legal-looking documents.*)

MRS. CARRINGTON. I planned to be on my way home this morning, but Ms. Prescott convinced me to have lunch with her.

ARTHUR. Ms. Prescott doesn't let much grass grow.

JESSICA. The concert tour will be a marvelous plug for the books. It's called synergy.

MRS. CARRINGTON. If he doesn't sell a few hundred copies at each performance I'll be amazed.

ARTHUR. I hope you're right.

MRS. CARRINGTON. No question about it.

JESSICA. You're marketable, Arthur.

ARTHUR. So is a tinned ham. (*GEORGE crosses to desk, puts down the documents, hands ARTHUR a pen.*)

MRS. CARRINGTON (*to JESSICA*). What is the first book going to be called? (*As MRS. CARRINGTON and JESSICA talk, ARTHUR considers the documents, GEORGE peers over his shoulder.*)

JESSICA. "State of Mind."
MRS. CARRINGTON. "State of Mind"? Yes, I like it. Does Mr. Sinclair reveal how he does his amazing act?
JESSICA. No. It's about how we only use fifty percent of our mental capabilities.
MRS. CARRINGTON (*intrigued*). Only fifty percent? You do have a certain *flair* for unsettling a person.
ARTHUR (*signing documents*). Here we go. There's one. (*Hands document to GEORGE.*) Two. (*Hands to GEORGE.*) Three. (*Hands to GEORGE.*) Four. (*Hands to GEORGE who returns it to him.*)
GEORGE. Your copy, Arthur. I'll keep two. And one for Mrs. Carrington. (*GEORGE goes to attache case, puts in two copies. He crosses behind sofa, handing one to MRS. CARRINGTON. She stands. Dialogue continues during this blocking.*)
JESSICA (*holding up large manila envelope*). I've had the publicity people work up some ideas based on the introduction to "State of Mind." Look them over, will you? (*She crosses to desk.*)
ARTHUR. You mean, now?
JESSICA (*handing ARTHUR the envelope*). Why not?
ARTHUR (*putting envelope down on desk*). Well, I'd like some time to think. It's an occasional habit of mine.
JESSICA (*smiling*). You've got all night. That should be sufficient.
MRS. CARRINGTON. I admire your tenaciousness, Jessica.
ARTHUR. I've got the first chapter to work on, as well. Suddenly, I'm feeling *pressured*.
GEORGE (*to JESSICA*). Ignore him. (*To MRS. CARRINGTON.*) I'll work up something more formal within the week. Until then, (*Indicating documents.*) this is your assurance that Arthur Sinclair will not escape your net.
MRS. CARRINGTON. My net? (*Chuckling.*) I'm not a butterfly hunter.
JESSICA. As far as Arthur Sinclair is concerned - you are a *big game* hunter.

Act II   MURDER BY NATURAL CAUSES   Page 37

MRS. CARRINGTON (*liking this idea*). Yes, I suppose I am. He's quite a trophy.
ARTHUR. I hope you're not planning on having me stuffed.
MRS. CARRINGTON (*chuckling*). It's a thought.
JESSICA (*to ARTHUR*). I have to get Mrs. Carrington back to her hotel.
MRS. CARRINGTON (*to GEORGE*). I appreciate everything you've done. You've been a great help.
GEORGE. My pleasure. If anything comes up I'll be in touch by phone.
MRS. CARRINGTON. Thank you again. (*She waves the contract at ARTHUR.*) I'm delighted this has worked out, Mr. Sinclair.
ARTHUR. You must call me Arthur.
MRS. CARRINGTON. Happy to. (*Girlishly.*) I bet you don't know my first name.
ARTHUR. It's Cornelia.
MRS. CARRINGTON. Sorry I asked. (*To GEORGE.*) I knew I'd have his signature before I left.
ARTHUR (*standing*). Is that why you had eggs Benedict for luncheon? To celebrate? (*MRS. CARRINGTON is wide-eyed, looks questioningly at JESSICA.*)
JESSICA. Don't look at me. I didn't tell him.
MRS. CARRINGTON. You had a spy at the restaurant?
ARTHUR. No, not at the restaurant. In your mind.
MRS. CARRINGTON (*delightedly*). You are a wizard, aren't you? Confess.
ARTHUR. You've been worrying about your cholesterol count all day.
MRS. CARRINGTON. Stop! Get out of my head, Mr. Sinclair. (*She moves UR, JESSICA follows behind her.*) Imagine being married to a man who can read your mind! It's terrifying. MRS. CARRINGTON exits UR. JESSICA calls back to ARTHUR as she goes out the door.)
JESSICA. I'll call you first thing in the morning, about breakfast. (*She exits UR.*)
ARTHUR. I would say every moment of my life for the next few years is accounted for.

GEORGE. Not complaining, I hope.

ARTHUR. Not in the least.

GEORGE. Ms. Prescott is eager to get the first book on the market as soon as possible. She's hoping they'll syndicate it in metropolitan newspapers. Prepublication. Builds up interest.

ARTHUR. She's quite a woman.

GEORGE. You're lucky when it comes to the ladies, Arthur. They always like you. A bachelor like me is wedded to his work. I envy you.

ARTHUR *(cautiously)*. Maybe I shouldn't mention this, but I saw your ex-wife yesterday.

GEORGE. It's all right. Louise and I are talking again, sometimes with her lawyers in the room.

ARTHUR. Any chance of reconciliation?

GEORGE. Doubtful.

ARTHUR. Sorry to hear that.

GEORGE. She left me the house, but she took everything else. Just hang onto Allison. She's one in a million.

ARTHUR. George, have dinner with me.

GEORGE. Here?

ARTHUR. Allison has a casserole heating up. I hope you won't mind low salt.

GEORGE. Well.

(ALLISON enters from UR in time to overhear these last lines. She's dressed for some "event." She steps to mirror, checking her appearance.)

ALLISON. Arthur, there's not enough for two.

ARTHUR. Marta can whip something up.

ALLISON. You know I gave her the night off.

ARTHUR. That's right. I forgot.

GEORGE. Listen, I appreciate the invitation, but it's been one of those days. All I want to do is go home and take off my tie.

ALLISON. We'll make it some other time.

GEORGE. Fine. Have a nice evening. *(He picks up his attache case, exits UR.)*

Act II MURDER BY NATURAL CAUSES Page 39

ARTHUR (*moving toward sofa*). Not too gracious of you.
ALLISON (*still looking in mirror*). Hmmmmm?
ARTHUR. George could use some company.
ALLISON. And you'll use any excuse not to work on your book.
ARTHUR. I know, I know.
ALLISON (*moving to him*). You made Mrs. Carrington - joyful.
ARTHUR. Hooray for Mrs. Carrington.
ALLISON. She was chattering like a contented monkey when she went out the door.
ARTHUR. I signed for the concert tour.
ALLISON. I knew you would. Mrs. Carrington's fascinated by you. (*Teasingly.*) I'll have to watch you two. I can be a jealous female.
ARTHUR (*pulling her to him*). I wish you didn't have to meet some people about opening a gallery. Who are they, anyway?
ALLISON. No one you'd be interested in. I'm sorry it came up last minute.
ARTHUR. I'm not even invited. I just pay for it.
ALLISON. Quit stalling and get to work. (*Kisses him gingerly.*) I'll be back as soon as I can.
ARTHUR (*playfully*). Scout's honor?
ALLISON (*smiling*). Scout's honor. (*Checks wristwatch.*) Oops, I'm running late. (*Moves UR.*) Love you. (*She exits UR. ARTHUR sighs. Crossing to desk, he picks up manila envelope, looking at it.*)
ARTHUR. All right, *urgent*. It's you and me and a warm casserole. (*He sits in chair in front of desk, pulling papers from envelope.*) Let's get to work. It's going to be - a long night. (*He begins to read. CURTAIN*)

SCENE TWO

AT RISE OF CURTAIN: *It is one hour later. The radio is on, playing something soft and restful. The door to the inner-den stands ajar, some light spilling out. GIL enters silently UR, wearing a stylish sport shirt and pants. He glances around the empty room. Moving to the antique table, he opens the drawer. The gun is in place. GIL takes the gun, checking the chamber for the blank.*

ARTHUR'S VOICE (*coming from den*). Allison? Is that you? (*GIL hurriedly returns the gun, closing the drawer.*) Who's there? (*GIL moves back UR, positioning himself as if he's just about to enter.*)

GIL (*calling out*). Uh, I'm sorry about the bell. I rang.

(*ARTHUR enters DR from inner-den, gripping some papers.*)

ARTHUR. Who are you? What are you doing in my house? (*He closes door to inner-den.*)

GIL (*moving down*). Don't get the wrong idea, Mr. Sinclair. I'm not a burglar or anything like that. My name is Gil Weston. I work for the "San Diego Dispatch." Didn't your wife tell you?

ARTHUR (*snapping off radio*). Tell me what?

GIL. Hey, I'm sorry. I thought you were expecting me. We had an appointment at eight o'clock.

ARTHUR. An appointment?

GIL. I called your wife last week. She said tonight would be a good time to come by.

ARTHUR. Come by for what?

GIL (*moving behind sofa*). You're doing a concert in San Diego on the fifteenth, aren't you? My paper would like something for the Sunday magazine section.

ARTHUR. You couldn't have come at a less convenient time, but it's my wife's fault. She never mentioned it.

GIL. I thought I heard your voice but I guess it was the radio announcer. The front door was unlocked. Maybe I should go out and come in again.

ARTHUR. Have we ever met? You look familiar.

GIL. A lot of people think that. (*Lowering his voice.*) "Caroline, are you telling me this is instant coffee?"

Act II MURDER BY NATURAL CAUSES Page 41

You know, the TV commercial. That's me, the guy at the breakfast table.
ARTHUR. You do commercials? I thought you were a reporter.
GIL. Actually I'm just a stringer for the San Diego paper. I do a lot of free-lance work here in L.A. An occasional TV commercial keeps me out of the unemployment line.
ARTHUR. An actor *and* a reporter? Unusual combination.
GIL. Just your average Renaissance man. Anything to survive.
ARTHUR. As long as you're here you might as well get your interview, but I can't spare much time. Is that understood?
GIL. Gotcha.
ARTHUR. How do you want to do this?
GIL *(indicating sofa)*. You make yourself comfortable, Mr. Sinclair. Don't pay any attention to me. I like to move around when I do an interview. *(ARTHUR shrugs, anxious to get it over with. Crossing to sofa, he sits.)*
ARTHUR. Proceed, Mr. Weston. *(As GIL conducts the interview he does, indeed, move around.)*
GIL. I'm sure people would like to know when you first discovered these *powers* you have. You were originally a magician, weren't you?
ARTHUR. In my distant youth, I had a mind-reading act with a young lady.
GIL. What became of her?
ARTHUR. Last I heard she had six children and was married to a used car dealer.
GIL. What did you use? Some kind of code?
ARTHUR. Trade secret. Anyway, one evening after the show I was reading the paper. There was a series of stranglings in St. Louis. *(By now, GIL is standing by the chair in front of the desk.)* For some strange reason I envisioned a left-handed man, someone who worked with animals. It was a powerful mental image. I called the police and told them about it. They thought it was

a publicity stunt. Four weeks later, they found the strangler. He was a maintenance man at the zoo. He was left-handed.

GIL. Unbelievable.

ARTHUR. That was only the beginning. My fake mind-reading act had become the real thing.

GIL. How long have you been married?

ARTHUR. Why?

GIL *(shrugging)*. No reason. Your wife sounded nice on the phone.

ARTHUR. Nice, but apparently forgetful. So am I. I haven't offered you a drink. What will you have. And don't ask me to read your mind.

GIL. A beer would be fine. *(ARTHUR goes to bar, stoops down and gets beer from unseen refrigerator.)*

ARTHUR. Glass?

GIL. Bottle's okay.

ARTHUR. Why don't you *punch up* your interview with some colorful background? Readers always like that.

GIL. What kind of colorful background? *(When the top is off the beer, ARTHUR crosses to GIL who meets him halfway, in front of sofa.)*

ARTHUR. You could say I've evolved from a long line of illustrious predecessors. Alchemists, soothsayers, witch doctors. *(Pause.)* Aren't you taking notes?

GIL. I've got a good memory. *(ARTHUR sits on sofa again.)* It's one thing to read people's minds from a stage. You can always hire somebody to check out the audience. Get their names and backgrounds and what they eat for breakfast. But that thing with the strangler - it's almost too good to be true.

ARTHUR. Are you hinting I'm a fake? It's documented. Made all the papers.

GIL. Trouble is, most of the reporters never bothered to verify the story. So when I got this assignment, I called the St. Louis police. Funny thing is, they don't remember you being involved.

ARTHUR. You must have talked with the wrong person.

GIL. The guy I talked with said he was in charge of the investigation.

Act II MURDER BY NATURAL CAUSES

ARTHUR (*annoyed*). How much longer do you think this is going to take?

GIL. This is a great house. (*Stepping to French doors, he points to indicate outside.*) I could see the pool when I drove up. Too bad you can't use it.

ARTHUR. Why do you say that?

GIL. Well, uh...your heart.

ARTHUR. There's nothing wrong with my heart. (*GIL takes a swallow of beer, puts bottle on top of desk.*) I have a pacemaker.

GIL. I wasn't sure you'd talk about it.

ARTHUR. I don't keep it a secret.

GIL. Guess you have to take it easy, though.

ARTHUR. Not at all.

GIL. Come on, Mr. Sinclair. A friend of mine had a heart attack and he can't even walk his dog.

ARTHUR. You're quite a skeptic, aren't you?

GIL. Hey, sorry I brought it up. I didn't mean to upset you. If you're worried about it, I won't mention it in the article.

ARTHUR (*irritated*). Either I'm not communicating clearly or you're not listening. (*Instructs.*) A weak heart doesn't have to be a disability. I can function as well as you.

GIL. Right.

ARTHUR. You don't believe me.

GIL. Well, maybe as well as most people. But I'm pretty athletic. And I'm, you know, younger than you are. No offense.

ARTHUR (*measuring him for a beat, then taking off his jacket*). Hold this. (*Hands it to GIL.*)

GIL. What are you going to do?

ARTHUR. Watch. (*ARTHUR begins to do push-ups in front of sofa. NOTE: If the push-ups prove difficult, consult Production Notes for alternative suggestions.*)

GIL. Hey Mr. Sinclair, take it easy, will you?

ARTHUR. ...four ...five ...six ...seven. Satisfied?

GIL. Yeah, great. You'd better stop.

ARTHUR (*resuming push-ups*). ...eight... nine... ten. (*Gradually, ARTHUR begins to tire. His breathing is loud and labored, but he keeps going.)... eleven... twelve. (Up and down, up and down.)*

GIL. You'll hurt yourself. Stop.

ARTHUR *(eager to prove his point)*. I haven't even started. How many can you do?

GIL. Maybe fifty, sixty. But I'm in condition. *(Suddenly, ARTHUR gasps and collapses. GIL puts the jacket on back of chair at desk, moves to ARTHUR, bends down. ARTHUR sounds like an asthmatic pipe organ.)* Mr. Sinclair! You okay? *(ARTHUR coughs. GIL helps him up.)* You'd better sit down. You don't look so good.

ARTHUR. Can't get my breath, that's all.

GIL. Don't talk.

ARTHUR. I'm fine, I tell you.

GIL. Take it easy. *(He eases ARTHUR onto the sofa, into a sitting position.)*

ARTHUR. Stupid thing for me to do, wasn't it? But I had to show you. It was a challenge.

GIL. Did I challenge you?

ARTHUR. Didn't you? Well, maybe not. If I could read minds, if I weren't a fake, as you seem to think, I'd say you never called the St. Louis police. Would I be correct? *(GIL doesn't answer.)* You need some convincing. *(He gets up, breathing somewhat easier, but still heavily. Crossing to his desk, he opens a drawer, takes out deck of playing cards.)* Over here, Mr. Weston. *(He gestures to front of desk. GIL crosses over.)* I'll see if I can make you less of a skeptic.

GIL. Card tricks?

ARTHUR. Hardly. The mind is what we're working with. *(ARTHUR slowly shuffles the cards. His breathing is now much easier.)* Would you say they're fairly shuffled?

GIL *(indifferently)*. I guess. *(ARTHUR hands him the deck.)*

ARTHUR. I want you to think of a card. Change your mind as often as you like.

GIL. Only one card?

Act II   MURDER BY NATURAL CAUSES   Page 45

ARTHUR. Only one. And not the ace of spades.
GIL. Why not?
ARTHUR. Too obvious. (*Pause.*) Got one?
GIL (*thinking*). Yes.
ARTHUR. Find it in the deck and put it on the desk. Face up. (*GIL looks through the deck, finds his card. Puts it on desk.*)
GIL. King of diamonds.
ARTHUR. King of diamonds? That was a free choice?
GIL. Wasn't it?
ARTHUR. Let's see. (*ARTHUR crosses to console, opens a cabinet drawer, looks for something inside. GIL puts down cards, picks up bottle of beer and sips. ARTHUR finds what he wants, holds it up.*) Here it is. An audio cassette.
GIL. So?
ARTHUR. Listen. (*He puts on the cassette and his own voice booms out. See Production Notes.*)
ARTHUR'S VOICE. "Good evening, this is Arthur Sinclair and we have just conducted an experiment in mental projection. The card you selected and removed from the deck was pre-ordained, by me. You had no other choice because I transmitted it to your mind. That's why, of course, you picked - the king of diamonds."
GIL. Hey, that's something else. Terrific. You actually made me think of that card!
ARTHUR. I couldn't send you home without a demonstration.
GIL (*easing into it*). You know, sometimes I think I can *tune in* on things.
ARTHUR. You probably can.
GIL. Really?
ARTHUR. It's not uncommon. Most people have the ability, but they don't know how to control it.
GIL. Funny you should say that. Because right now, while we're talking, this - mental picture keeps floating into my head.
ARTHUR. What do you see?
GIL. Forget it. It's ridiculous.

ARTHUR (*intrigued; moves in front of sofa*). No. Tell me.

GIL. Well, for some reason I get the feeling there's... a gun in this house. (*ARTHUR doesn't like this and it shows on his face.*) Am I right? (*ARTHUR nods.*) I knew it! Isn't that strange? Let's see if I can get anything else. (*He presses his fingers to his forehead.*). It's a .38. No, a .22. You keep it upstairs, in the bedroom.

ARTHUR. Now just a minute! How did you know that?

GIL (*laughing*). Fooled you, didn't I?

ARTHUR (*off-balance*). What?

GIL. Your wife told me. We got to talking when I called and she mentioned there were a lot of robberies in the neighborhood. I said she should get a gun.

ARTHUR. And, she told you we already had one.

GIL. Uh-huh. She didn't sound too happy about having it in the house. I guess that's how you do it. I mean, read minds. Pick up random information on the sly.

ARTHUR. Don't think me rude, Mr. Weston, but I must get back to my work.

GIL. I'm fast to catch on. I'm a quick study. (*He strides to console, rummages through the cabinet drawers.*)

ARTHUR (*sharply*). What do you think you're doing?

GIL (*finding what he's looking for*). I thought so. (*He holds up a few tape cassettes, lets them drop to the floor.*)

ARTHUR. Stop that.

GIL. Fifty-two cassettes. One for every card in the deck. As soon as you see my card, you come over here and pick out the right tape.

ARTHUR (*coldly*). Get out. Now.

GIL. Don't I get a chance to show you what I can do? (*Puts his fingertips to his temples mocking ARTHUR'S mind-reading routine.*) For instance, upstairs - in your bedroom - there's a red and yellow quilt.

ARTHUR (*shocked*). What!

GIL. Pillowcases with your monogram on them. What else, hmmmm? I see a green chair - a dressing table.

Act II   MURDER BY NATURAL CAUSES   Page 47

ARTHUR. You went through the house before you came in here.
GIL. You're not even close. Got you going, haven't I? Okay, I'll let you in on the secret. *(Lowers hands.)* A few months ago your house was in one of those decorating magazines.
ARTHUR *(breathing a sign of relief)*. You looked at the pictures.
GIL. Uh-huh. Simple when you know how to read minds, isn't it?
ARTHUR *(something suddenly occurring to him)*. Wait a minute.
GIL. I'm one step ahead of you. You remembered there weren't any pictures of the bedroom. Maybe I *am* a mind reader.
ARTHUR. All right, Mr. Weston. You've had your fun. Time to go.
GIL. I haven't finished my demonstration.
ARTHUR. That's what you think.
GIL. You'll miss the best part. *(ARTHUR crosses to desk, picks up telephone receiver.)*
ARTHUR. If you don't leave, I'm calling the police.
GIL. But the best part is about your wife.
ARTHUR *(hesitating)*. What about her?
GIL. Name's Allison. Quite attractive. She was working in an art gallery when you met her.
ARTHUR *(not impressed)*. You could have read that anywhere.
GIL. True. But where would I read she has a birthmark on her lower back? A birthmark she doesn't want people to know about.
ARTHUR *(slamming down receiver)*. *How did you know!*
GIL. I saw it there.
ARTHUR. That's a lie!
GIL. Is it? *(Moves behind sofa.)* I said the gun was upstairs. I was wrong. *(Fingertips to temples.)* I get the impression it's right here in this room. *(As ARTHUR reacts.)* Where, oh, where? *(Points to inner-den.)* In there, I think. *(Takes a step right, stops.)* No. *(Turns to desk.)* It's the desk. *(Takes step toward desk.)* No.

(*Points to console.*) In there. No, no. (*Fingertips to temples.*) Where, oh, where?

ARTHUR. You're being childish!

GIL. Let me convince you. (*Points to antique table.*) There. It's there!

ARTHUR. Nonsense. (*GIL crosses to antique table, takes out gun, holds it up.*)

GIL. Surprise, surprise!

ARTHUR. What in the name of heaven?

GIL. Still don't get it, do you? By now, I thought you'd be picking up my vibrations. (*Motions to sofa with gun.*) Over there. I don't know what you've got in the desk. I'm not taking any chances. *Move!* (*ARTHUR obeys, moves to sofa.*) Sit. (*ARTHUR does.*) In case you haven't read my mind, I'm going to kill you.

ARTHUR (*horrified*). It's a joke, isn't it? Someone's put you up to this? (*As GIL moves about the room, he keeps the gun trained on the bewildered ARTHUR.*)

GIL. Let's see, you're upstairs, most of the lights down here are off. (*He snaps off a lamp, then another.*) You hear a sound, you call, "Allison." No answer. You hear something. There's someone down here. Someone's broken into the house.

ARTHUR. Listen to me, please.

GIL. So what do you do? You take the gun from the bedside table and come downstairs. You're a little frightened. (*He's at the desk, pulling out drawers, scattering cards to the floor.*) It could be your imagination. You come into this room. Look around. And then, the guy who's here, the guy who's robbing your house, he panics. If he runs, you'll shoot him. So he decides to jump you. That makes sense, doesn't it? (*GIL tips over desk lamp, pulls a picture or some books from the wall.*)

ARTHUR (*petrified*). Please.

GIL. There has to be a scuffle. (*He steps to chair in front of desk, tips it over. ARTHUR is still petrified, his hand goes to his heart.*) The two of you fight back and forth. (*He goes behind sofa, throws some magazines from table to floor. He moves to chair in front of inner-*

Act II MURDER BY NATURAL CAUSES Page 49

den, pushes it over.) And then... then... the gun goes off. *(He steps to sofa, leans toward ARTHUR, puts the muzzle of gun to his chest.)* Point-blank range. Have to leave powder burns. You understand.

ARTHUR *(choking)*. Don't.

GIL *(finger tightening on trigger, pauses)*. Oops, how do you like that - I'm getting careless. *(He crosses to desk for beer bottle.)* Wouldn't do for our thief in the night to be having a drink with you. *(With one eye on ARTHUR, GIL takes a handkerchief from his pocket, wiping away his prints on the bottle. ARTHUR is breathing heavily again. GIL'S performance is taking its toll. ARTHUR claws at his collar, loosens his shirt.)*

ARTHUR. Look, whoever you are, I can get you money. All the money you want, anything you want.

GIL. It's not what I want. It's what Allison wants. It has to be.

ARTHUR. You'll never get away with it. *(He presses his hand to his heart.)* They'll find out.

GIL. Ordinary breaking and entering happens all the time. I'll jimmy the lock when I leave. Those tapes? I'll have to wipe off my prints. *(GIL steps in front of sofa. ARTHUR is in such a bad way, GIL considers him no threat. But in a sudden burst, ARTHUR lunges, tackling GIL from behind. GIL, knocked off balance, goes sprawling. The gun drops to the floor. They struggle, roll about, attempting to grab the gun. Finally, ARTHUR has it. GIL jumps up, trying to kick gun from ARTHUR'S grip. ARTHUR fires! GIL recoils. Giving a low spiralling moan, he clutches his midsection, slips to floor and dies. ARTHUR struggles to his feet. Dazed, he stares down at the body. Then he looks at the gun in his hand, lets it fall to the floor as if it were something unclean. We hear the sound of the front door slamming.)*

ALLISON. Arthur!

(A couple of moments pass. ALLISON enters UR, running into the room.)

ARTHUR (*struggling for breath*). He tried to kill me! (*ALLISON is horrified. She expected to find her husband's body on the floor and here he is, "alive!" She steps to GIL'S body, her eyes widen, she covers her mouth.*)

ALLISON. Oh, no!

ARTHUR. You know him, don't you! The two of you were lovers. You wanted to murder me! You left the door unlocked, you brought the gun downstairs.

ALLISON. I don't know what you're talking about. All right, I knew him. But that was a long time ago. I told him I never wanted to see him again. (*Looks down.*) You're sure he's dead?

ARTHUR. I don't know and I don't care. (*ALLISON kneels by the body, forces herself to feel for a pulse. A long pause. She glances up at ARTHUR, shakes her head, crosses to telephone and picks it up.*) Who are you calling?

ALLISON. The police.

ARTHUR. Are you out of your mind?

ALLISON. We have to report it.

ARTHUR. Don't you understand? I shot him.

ALLISON. It was self-defense.

ARTHUR. That's not the point... (*He breaks off, a look of pain on his face. His hand goes to his chest.*)

ALLISON. What's wrong?

ARTHUR. ...Chest pains. (*He stumbles back onto sofa.*)

ALLISON. Where did you put your medicine?

ARTHUR. Upstairs...bedroom.

ALLISON. I'll get it. Don't move. (*She runs out, UR.*) (*ARTHUR takes several deep breaths, gets unsteadily to his feet. His throat dry, he crosses to bar for water. Trembling, he manages a few sips. He moves to mirror above console, straightens up and looks at himself. While ARTHUR'S attention is on mirror, GIL rises. In crouched position, he gets behind ARTHUR. Slowly rising, he puts a hand to his shoulder. ARTHUR sees GIL'S reflection, cries out, horror stricken, turns. He lunges across room, stumbling, terrified. By the desk, his body goes rigid, eyes roll, both hands clutch at his*

Act II MURDER BY NATURAL CAUSES Page 51

heart. GIL stares at him, not daring to breathe. We wait for ARTHUR'S death rattle. Instead, he stops gasping, his body relaxes. He begins to laugh. Within seconds, he is calm and totally composed. GIL is speechless. ARTHUR claps a few times in mock applause.)

ARTHUR. Good show, Mr. Weston. My compliments. The hand on the shoulder was a marvelous touch.

GIL. W-w-what...

ARTHUR. But then I thought I was rather convincing myself. Unless you think all that heavy breathing was overdone. *(He goes behind desk, sets the chair back in position and sits.)*

GIL. You... knew.

ARTHUR. Of course I knew. But that didn't detract from your performance. Take my word for it, those reviews of your play were unfair. Anytime you need a testimonial...

GIL. Shut up!

ARTHUR. Watch your manners, young man. You're in a great deal of trouble.

(ALLISON dashes into room from UR. She looks at ARTHUR with astonishment.)

ARTHUR *(brightly)*. Come in, dear. Ah, you forgot my medicine. No matter. As you can see - I've made a miraculous recovery.

ALLISON *(looking at GIL)*. How did this happen?

GIL. What difference does it make? He knew everything before I even got here.

ALLISON. That's not possible. You must have given it away. *(She steps to right of sofa.)*

ARTHUR. Don't be critical, Allison. He followed your game plan perfectly... *(To GIL.)*... although she should have told you that I do a hundred push-ups every day.

GIL. You're enjoying this.

ARTHUR *(with contempt)*. Immensely. *(He moves in front of desk, speaks to ALLISON.)* You would have been proud of him. He was brilliant. (*To GIL.*) I was supposed to think I shot you. If *that* didn't do me in, there was always your return from the dead. (*To ALLISON.*) What were you going to do when I expired? Call the paramedics and weep about my unexpected coronary? (*ALLISON sits on arm of sofa, very cool.*)

ALLISON. Something like that.

ARTHUR. You'd send him home first, of course. Clean up the mess. Really, Allison, I'm impressed. Very ingenious.

ALLISON. How did you find out?

ARTHUR. You ignored the first rule of infidelity, darling. Never cheat on a man who employs a private detective.

ALLISON (*understanding*). Eddie Oakman.

ARTHUR. The invisible man. He told me about you two months ago.

ALLISON. You never said a word.

ARTHUR (*moving DC*). I was much too fascinated by your - what shall I call it - curious behavior? Sudden interest in my health. Questions about our joint stock holdings. The tearful request for a gun because of all the robberies in the neighborhood. That's when I started listening in on your phone calls.

ALLISON. That's contemptible. Then you knew it was going to be tonight.

ARTHUR. I *thought* it would be. Particularly when the gun moved itself downstairs and you gave Marta last night and *tonight* off. Your last minute business appointment.

GIL. What are we going to do?

ARTHUR. I suggest you get the hell out of my house before I have you charged with attempted murder.

ALLISON. You'd better do as he says.

GIL. I don't want to leave you alone with him. (*Glances at gun, with a promising thought.*) It could still work. Not the heart attack, but the breaking and entering. He could be shot during the burglary.

ALLISON. That's no good.

GIL. Why?

Act II   MURDER BY NATURAL CAUSES   Page 53

ARTHUR. Tell him, darling.

ALLISON. I'm here. I don't have an alibi.

ARTHUR. Not very clever when you're doing your own planning, are you Mr. Weston? I'll give you another reason your idea's no good. *(He steps to desk, takes a folded sheet of paper from a drawer, holds it out.)* Read it. *(GIL doesn't move.)* Do you want me to read it for you? *(GIL crosses over, snatches away paper, unfolds and reads it.)* Out loud. Your partner in crime might be interested.

ALLISON. What does it say?

GIL. "To the authorities. If anything happens to me, including my death by natural causes, it will be as a result of a plot between my wife and her lover, Gilbert Weston." *(ALLISON furiously crosses to GIL, grabs the paper, reads.)*

ARTHUR. You'll notice that's a carbon copy. The original is with my publisher. To be opened and read if I'm not alive and kicking tomorrow morning. *(ALLISON crumples the paper.)* If you've got any sense at all, Mr. Weston, you'll get out of this house.

GIL *(to ALLISON)*. Come with me.

ALLISON. No. I'll be all right.

GIL. I'm not leaving without you.

ARTHUR. I approve of gallantry. There's not enough of it in the world. Bravo, Mr. Weston. *(GIL still doesn't move.)*

ALLISON. I'll talk to you in the morning, Gil. *(GIL looks at ALLISON, then at ARTHUR, then back at ALLISON. Completely frustrated, he storms out UR. ALLISON is the picture of control, sitting on sofa, crossing legs nonchalantly. ARTHUR moves around, turns on lamps GIL turned off.)*

ARTHUR. Do we kiss and make up? *(Bitterly.)* Or do you tell me how sorry you are?

ALLISON. Why did you let us go through with it?

ARTHUR. Leverage. I want to be rid of you just as much as you want to be rid of me. *(She stiffens, quickly recovers.)*

ALLISON. That is a surprise. You're full of surprises, aren't you, Arthur?
ARTHUR. Have I offended your vanity? Tsk, tsk. It's simple enough. I don't want to pay for the privilege of getting rid of you. You'll get your divorce. But you'll waive all rights to alimony, community property, any kind of settlement. You came to me with nothing and that's the way you're leaving.
ALLISON. I'm not sure I like those conditions.
ARTHUR. I suggest you accept my terms.
ALLISON (*holding up crumpled note*). And this?
ARTHUR. Don't worry about it. A small precaution in case your friend got carried away.
ALLISON. The original's not with your publisher?
ARTHUR. Hardly. That would be embarrassing for both of us. I destroyed the original. (*Sound of doorbell. They look UR.*) He's not stupid enough to come back here, is he? (*Another sound of doorbell. ARTHUR exits UR. ALLISON crosses to desk, puts crumpled note in ashtray and with match or cigarette lighter, burns note. See Production Notes.*)

GEORGE'S VOICE (*from offstage UR*). I am sorry to bother you, Arthur. I won't take long. I know you're working.

(*ALLISON leans against desk, faces UR. GEORGE and ARTHUR enter.*)

GEORGE. A few details about your contract with Mrs. Carrington. (*Looks about, sees disorder.*)
ARTHUR. Actually, I'm glad you came by. You have an impeccable sense of timing. It's always nice to have a witness. (*GEORGE spots gun, moves toward it. ARTHUR crosses to left of sofa.*) George is wondering what happened here, darling. Do you want to tell him? Or shall I do the honors? (*ALLISON remains frozen in place.*) Allison tried to kill me tonight. (*No reaction from GEORGE.*) Didn't you hear what I said?
GEORGE. I heard. (*To ALLISON.*) What went wrong?

Act II MURDER BY NATURAL CAUSES Page 55

ALLISON. He found out about Gil months ago. Tonight was a setup.

ARTHUR *(confused)*. What is this? What are you two talking about?

GEORGE. Did he call the police?

ALLISON. No.

GEORGE. Then there's no harm done. *(He takes a glove from his pocket, puts it on. ARTHUR stares, bewildered.)* I was hoping the other way would work, Arthur. I really was. But there's one trouble with trying to induce a heart attack - it's not very dependable.

ARTHUR. You know about that?

GEORGE. Oh, yes. And it would have been very clean. No gun, no bullets. Death by cardiac arrest.

ARTHUR *(beginning to understand)*. Then you two... all along... *(GEORGE takes out a pen, bends down, inserts it into the muzzle of gun. Lifting gun from floor carefully to avoid smudging Gil's fingerprints, he returns pen to pocket.)* What are you doing?

GEORGE. Alternatives, Arthur. The heart attack approach was a long shot. If it worked, fine - but we never counted on it. Naturally we have a fallback position.

ALLISON. I'll be in the car.

ARTHUR *(frightened)*. Allison! *(ALLISON exits UR. Desperately, ARTHUR moves toward GEORGE DC.)* George, we've been friends too long.

GEORGE. I wish it didn't have to be this way. I know you don't believe that, but it's true.

ARTHUR. It won't work. That young man, Weston, he'll go to the police.

GEORGE. No, they'll go to him. That's far enough, Arthur. *(ARTHUR stops.)* His fingerprints are all over this gun. And we both know he can't account for his whereabouts tonight.

ARTHUR *(frantically)*. He'll tell them about Allison.

GEORGE. A wild and ridiculous story about a conspiracy to frighten you to death? Who will believe him? Besides, Allison has a perfect alibi. She was *with me* during the murder. At my house. Telling me about her terribly jealous and unstable lover. I'm advising her to come home and warn you. Unfortunately, she'll be too late. (*He raises gun.*)

ARTHUR. You won't do it, George. I know you won't. (*Steps toward GEORGE.*) You can't. (*GEORGE fires! ARTHUR jerks back, pitches forward, clutching chest, collapses to rug in front of sofa, dead. GEORGE works rapidly. He lets gun drop to floor, peels off glove, pockets it as he moves UR. He snaps switch and some lamps go off, leaving the room in shadowy darkness. He exits UR. CURTAIN*)

SCENE THREE

AT RISE OF CURTAIN: *Later. The room is the same as at the end of preceding scene with one notable exception. ARTHUR'S body is gone. Also, the gun is missing. In a moment we hear the sound of front door opening. Seconds pass and ALLISON enters UR, house keys in hand. She steps quickly to phone, dials. She doesn't look at killing spot. There is a pause while she waits for her call to be answered.*

ALLISON (*into mouthpiece*). George. Yes, I'm fine. No hitch. I stopped at a gas station on my way home for cigarettes. I made certain the attendant noticed me. I asked him to make some change. I got there just as he was closing up, so he'll remember the time. I'm calling the police about my horrifying *discovery* right now. (*ALLISON hangs up, perfectly self-assured. Anxious for a look, she steps toward sofa, looks to floor. Not seeing the corpse, she gasps, hand to her mouth in terror. She looks behind sofa, etc., steps back to telephone, dials in panic.*) George, George, something's gone wrong. The body isn't here! Don't tell me to be calm. How can I be calm? No, no, I'm not hysterical. I tell you the body's *not* here. How do I

Act II MURDER BY NATURAL CAUSES Page 57

know where it is! You're the one who killed him. What'll we do!

(The sound of ARTHUR'S VOICE booms out from direction of inner-den. It only takes a few seconds to realize we are listening to a recorded voice. For an alternative suggestion, consult Production Notes.)

ARTHUR'S VOICE. Of all the illusions in the world of magic, there's one in particular that no magician could ever perform - returning from the dead. (*ALLISON can't believe her ears. She turns toward sound. Completely distracted by voice, she puts down receiver, braces herself.*) Many tried. None succeeded. Including Houdini, who promised his loving wife he would come back to her from the other side, but she waited in vain. (*ALLISON now realizes the voice is a recording. She takes a step forward.*)

ALLISON (*barely audibly*). It's a recording. (*Calls.*) Who's in there!

ARTHUR'S VOICE. As a mentalist, this is not my area of expertise. But I do make predictions, and I have a strong feeling that someone *will* return from the dead in the very near future. Perhaps tonight.

ALLISON (*over her shock*). Answer me. (*She takes another step. When door to den opens from the inside, she stops. There is a dramatic pause, followed by appearance of ARTHUR.*)

ARTHUR. Hello, Allison. I've been rehearsing a new lecture. Do you like it?

ALLISON (*uneasily*). He killed you. (*Adamantly.*) *He killed you*!

ARTHUR. Not quite. He *shot* me. There's a difference. There was nothing in the gun but blanks. You put in one for Mr. Weston and five live bullets. I took out the five rounds and replaced them with five blanks.

ALLISON. You... knew.

ARTHUR. Another lesson in infidelity, darling. If a private detective can find out about lover A... he can also find out about lover B.

ALLISON. So Eddie told you. But, why didn't you *say* anything?

ARTHUR. Because George and I have been friends for years. I was hoping that would mean something.

ALLISON. I don't understand.

ARTHUR. No. I don't suppose you do. I had the foolish idea that he wouldn't be able to go through with it. That at the last minute he couldn't pull the trigger. He must love you very much.

ALLISON. He does.

ARTHUR. Apparently. He even let you have a relationship with another man. But that had a practical purpose, didn't it? You both needed a scapegoat.

ALLISON. I've underestimated you. Congratulations. However, there's nothing further to be accomplished here. Good-bye, Arthur. (*She starts for the hallway, UR.*)

ARTHUR. Running back to George?

ALLISON. None of your business.

ARTHUR. I wonder if you've used him, too?

ALLISON. Wonder all you like.

ARTHUR. Allison. (*As she pauses.*) This isn't over yet.

ALLISON. Isn't it? Nothing happened here tonight. Nothing you can prove. It's our word against yours.

ARTHUR. Oh? (*He takes audio tape from pocket, holds it up.*) I showed Mr. Weston a trick. You know the one - select a card and my recorded voice will prove you had no free will about the selection.

ALLISON. I always thought that stunt was beneath you.

ARTHUR. Did you? And you never said a word. That's loyalty. But I haven't explained the *real* trick. *I left the tape running*. It's all here. Mr. Weston's voice. Your voice. George's. Mine. I'll play it for you. (*He steps to console, starts to play the tape.*)

ALLISON. There's no need. You surprise me, Arthur. You can't use that in court. It's not admissible evidence.

ARTHUR. Learn your law, darling. Recorded evidence *is* admissible in this state if it's related to the commission of any felony involving violence. I think

Act II   MURDER BY NATURAL CAUSES   Page 59

tonight qualifies. Don't you? (*He slips the tape from the console and pockets it.*)

ALLISON. What are you going to do?

ARTHUR (*pleasantly*). I thought you were leaving.

ALLISON (*intensely*). What are you going to do?

ARTHUR. I have three - what was George's word - alternatives. Sit down, Allison. (*ALLISON sags into a chair.*) One... I can send this tape to Mr. Weston. He's a rather violent young man. I'd hate to be in your shoes, or George's, if he finds out that he was your mutual puppet. (*ALLISON winces.*) You don't look well, dear. (*Cheerfully.*) Two... I can give the tape to the police. You and George will be arrested and tried. (*The fight's gone out of ALLISON. She just sits there. ARTHUR takes a handkerchief from his pocket and then a bullet. He carefully picks up the gun, ejects the clip and inserts the bullet.*)

ALLISON (*apprehensively*). What are you doing?

ARTHUR. Alternative number three - and by the way, this is a real bullet, not a blank - what's to stop me from killing you?

ALLISON. You can't be serious.

ARTHUR. Think about it. Gil's fingerprints are still on this gun. If he can be framed for *my* murder, why not yours? (*Smiles.*) Same frame - different victim.

ALLISON. Arthur--

ARTHUR. It all works out rather nicely. He came here tonight and pleaded with you to divorce me. You refused, and the two of you had a fight. You got the gun. He took it away.

ALLISON. He'll tell the police you were here!

ARTHUR. As George said, who will believe him? Especially if I have an alibi.

ALLISON. But you *don't* have an alibi.

ARTHUR. Oh, but I might. Remember Ms. Prescott, my editor? Suppose, just for the sake of argument, that she's in love with me, and that she'll swear I spent the night with her.

ALLISON. You're lying!

ARTHUR. Am I?

ALLISON. It doesn't matter. George knows.
ARTHUR. But he can't tell the truth, can he? Not as long as I have this tape. Think of the fun I'll have with good old George over the coming years. (*He sits down on right arm of sofa, aiming gun at ALLISON, taking a barrel sight. She stares at him, afraid.*) Three alternatives - which one should it be?
ALLISON. W-what are you going to do? (*No answer.*) Arthur, tell me!
ARTHUR (*smiling*). I have a suggestion for you, darling. (*A pause.*) Why don't you read my mind?

CURTAIN

PRODUCTION NOTES

SYNOPSIS OF SCENES: All of the action of the play takes place in the very elegant study/den of Arthur Sinclair's home in Beverly Hills, California. The time is the present, in the summer season. Act One, Scene One: a summer evening; Scene Two: afternoon, a few days later; Scene Three: the following night. Act Two, Scene One: Monday evening; Scene Two: one hour later; Scene Three: still later.

SETTING: DR is a door that leads into an adjacent room, which is actually an "inner-den." R, against the wall, is a handsome console cabinet with some drawers. The console has stereo equipment; TV, tape cassette, radio, etc. There's a mirror on the wall above the console.

Moving upstage, beyond the console cabinet, angled to audience view, is a bar. Behind the bar, out of sight, is a small refrigerator. On the wall are some shelves with assorted glasses and bottles.

UR is the entrance to an unseen hallway or alcove that leads to other areas of the house. There's a light switch near the entrance.

The UC wall is lined with book shelves. The volumes on the shelves are expensively bound and rich-looking. The book shelves are punctuated by some large theatrical posters that advertise famous "mentalists" and stage "illusionists" of the past, e.g., "Dunninger," "Houdini," "Dante."

UL is a small antique table with a drawer. L are French doors that open onto the grounds. There are drapes that can be pulled across. DL there's a desk with a chair behind it. Another chair is in front. There's a telephone on the desk, pen, lamp, ashtray, matches.

C, downstage somewhat, is a sofa. Behind the sofa is a table.

In front of the DR door there's a comfortable chair with a low table set on the downstage side.

To these basics should be added rug(s), lamps, additional stage dressing, maybe stools at the bar, more book shelves. On the wall behind the desk is another good spot for poster illustrating some magician or occultist, e.g. "Chung Lin Soo," "Thurston," "Mandrake," "Levante," etc.

Overall, the room is comfy, masculine and warm. Judging from the furnishings, there is no doubt that the man who lives in this house is wealthy. The posters tell us he's interested in the "strange."

PROPERTIES: Act One, Scene One: Robe, empty cigarette pack (GIL), wristwatch (ALLISON).

Act One, Scene Two: Large floral arrangement (pre-set), pipe (GEORGE), legal contract (ARTHUR), empty tray and same tray with hors d'oeuvres (MARTA), crushed cigarette pack (same as Scene One - ARTHUR), note pad (EDDIE), newspaper (MARTA).

Act One, Scene Three: 8 x 10 glossy photograph (MARTA), newspaper reviews, pack of cigarettes (GIL).

Act Two, Scene One: Large manila envelope with papers (JESSICA), attache case with four legal documents.

Act Two, Scene Two: Gun (pre-set in antique table drawer), glove, pen (GEORGE).

Act Two, Scene Three: House keys (ALLISON), thin glove, bullet in handkerchief, gun (ARTHUR).

COSTUMES and CHARACTERS:

GIL WESTON is a good looking young man, possessed of rough charm and arrogant self-interest. He can be captivating and irresistible. In Act One, Scene One, he wears a stylish robe: Act One, Scene Three; a rumpled sweat shirt and jeans, and in Act Two, Scene Two; a nice looking sport shirt and pants.

ALLISON SINCLAIR is a beautiful, sophisticated woman. She is cool, poised, intelligent and lively. She is always beautifully dressed, but appropriate to the occasion and time of day. Her hostess gown for the garden party should be especially lavish and becoming.

ARTHUR SINCLAIR is a handsome, worldly man. He is also shrewd with a somewhat theatrical manner. He wears expensive but casual clothes.

GEORGE BRUBAKER is a pleasant looking but rather nondescript man. He wears very good quality, conservative suits.

JESSICA PRESCOTT is an attractive young woman. She dresses in chic businesswoman fashion, rather tailored.

MARTA is a plain woman. In Act One, Scene Two, she should be attired in a conservative maid's uniform. In Act One, Scene Three, she wears a tacky, thin, topcoat and a silly looking hat. The general impression is frumpy.

EDDIE OAKMAN is a street-wise but rather uneducated man. He wears the same very out-of-date suit in each scene. He is a bit on the plump side.

MRS. CARRINGTON, is a middle aged woman but tries unsuccessfully to act younger than she is. In Act One, Scene Two, she wears a large hat, gloves, and a dressy, full, summer frock. In Act Two, Scene Two, she also wears matching hat and gloves and a dressy suit or dress.

All costumes are contemporary and appropriate to time and scene in the script unless otherwise noted.

MISCELLANEOUS NOTES: When Allison burns the incriminating note, be sure that the ashtray is deep. A decorative bowl is also a wise prop. For extra safety, it's a good idea to have a flower vase on the desk with water in it.

In regard to Arthur's recorded voice; the recordings should be played over the backstage audio system and fed into the auditorium. This way the voice is always loud and commanding.

If the director prefers, Arthur can actually *speak* his lines from the inner den in the opening moments of Act Two, Scene Three. The actor should recite the lines loudly. If the lines are spoken rather than played as a recording... Allison's line "It's a recording!" will be cut.

It is wise to have a cover in case the gun does not go off onstage as planned. To do this, have a gunmaster positioned offstage with a second gun loaded with blanks. He gets as close to the action as possible without being seen. If the actor pulls the onstage trigger and nothing happens, the gunmaster will immediately cover by firing.

Arthur's push-ups will depend on the physical capability of the actor. If the push-ups are too difficult... simply have the number to be done reduced. Or perform "modified" push-ups. Or, devise an exercise the actor is comfortable with and can easily manage.